MW00423631

THE
POSTMODERN
POET

HIMEROS & ANTEROS

The Postmodern Poet: Himeros & Anteros
© 2022 by Josiah Macrae Callaghan

All rights reserved under International Copyright Law.
Contents and/or cover may not be reproduced in whole or
in part in any form without the express written consent
of the publisher.

Paberback ISBN: 978-1-7370394-6-4
     ePub ISBN: 978-1-7370394-7-1

Library of Congress Control Number (LCCN): 2022910778

Good Soil Press
St. Paul, Minnesota

Cover and interior design:
The Brand Office

Cover Art: "Virgil's Tomb with a View of the Bay of Naples
in the Moonlight." Carl Georg Anton Graeb (1816-1864).
Open Access, Public Domain Usage from the Metropolitan
Musuem of Art, New York City.

JOSIAH MACRAE CALLAGHAN

THE

POSTMODERN

POET

HIMEROS & ANTEROS

Good Soil Press

"Callaghan offers the lyrical catharsis of an old soul, kidnapped from some ancient utopia, held hostage here in the dystopian now. This collection documents the melodious struggle of one enthralled by ideals of life and love, but who now must scratch and struggle to enjoy life and love as it comes to him here in the actual world. Readers who enjoy classic verse and clever abstraction will adore this fine collection."

—Dan Kent, author of *The Fundamentals of Skywriting*, *Diamonds Mixed with Broken Glass*, and *Tender Lines of Code*

"Raw, soul-rending, vulnerable—are but a few sentiments that rise up in the reader of Callaghan's compelling debut collection. *The Postmodern Poet* is verse that is at once lyrical when in the proximity of abiding love—*'the weaver of a strangely urgent thread'*—or a *'bloodletting nearly fatal'* in its felt void and longing. This is a work of a self-confessed romantic, a coming-of-age voice that demands of God either *'complete absence or total presence'* even as it heralds at last a full-throated celebratory faith that *'Love never dies!'* I look forward to more of what this promising artiste du langage has yet to herald."

—D.J. Rohling, author of *Ford's Crossing* (formerly *Ashes, Ashes*) and soon-to-be-released, *Rainie Hart*

"God has inspired every first-rate work of art,

though its subject may be utterly and entirely secular."

—SIMONE WEIL, *Waiting for God*

Dedication

To Meema—Katherine Beth Callaghan

VOLUME ONE IN THE

POSTMODERN POET SERIES:
HIMEROS & ANTEROS

CONTENTS

FOREWORD

SOME TIME AGO, amid the swelling crests of autumn's Aurelian aura, I found myself awash in something singularly beautiful and sorrowful. A melancholic melody wherein I was haunted by a deep sadness. Journeying up into the Coloradoan mountains, to a place above a floating haze of clouds, I first encountered Susanne Sundfør's soul-stirring *Self Portrait* album.[1] It was an original score, composed for a documentary about Norwegian photographer, Lene Marie Fossen. Each track archived the sufferings of a woman who bore the weight of a disease that literally ate away at her body, thieving the innocence of her childhood, besieging her from an early age. In her adulthood, Fossen would eventually succumb to her ailment, yet all along the way, she lived a life of bravery and artistry. Through the finesse of film and photography, Fossen captured those eternal moments

---

1. Susanne Sundfør, *Self-Portrait Original Soundtrack*, n.d., Bella Union 1017, 2020. MP3.

found only in the portraits of strangers and other lost, fragile souls. It gave me pause. I began to wonder about my own adolescence, before chronic depression's arrival. My early years were good ones, of free-spirited naivety and dreamworlds. A carefree life of boyhood, where the mind unraveled mental escapades in myth and fantasy, literature, creative capacity, and unassuming conversations with God. If I had been similarly deprived of my own sentimental youth, would I have carried on into the darker years with the strength and endurance that Fossen demonstrated during her physical suffering? I'm not too sure. The seasons that followed were dark indeed. I now look back upon the innocent age of my youth and consider the pleasant souvenirs from that time as gifts that would carry me through all my personal trials: spiritual, cognitive and ultimately, relational. The escapism of my imaginative, younger self and its world-building ideals would guide me through a new kind of pain that I would learn all about as a young man.

This collection of thoughts gathered as I traveled up a series of windy switchbacks into the Anthracite Range. Even the grandeur of the mountains, draped in golden Aspen groves could not detract or distract from the sublime melodies of Sundfør's album. All of it, the music, the skies, and nature's presentation, coalesced into a condensed mixture of emotions that spoke a strange reassuring sadness to me. Riding the coattails of a heartbreak that had thrown me into disillusionment, I felt that this music expressed a sorrow over lost innocence. It echoed a feeling of bereavement I was grappling with. Sundfør's melodies were like a memorial for lost things and during the past two years, I'd felt as if I had lost a great deal.

Winding my car through the summits and valleys west of Crested Butte, I encountered the final track of this perfect piece of pure art, "Amor Est Mortis."[2] Composed in a harmonious gothic style reminiscent of the old Latin hymns, it was a most fitting anthem to the poems I had begun slowly harvesting from my thoughts and experiences. Sung like a dirge, the simple and repetitive statement that *love is dead* seemed rather emblematic of what I was observing in our culture's increasingly dubious stance towards love and grand, essentialist narratives about Truth and Beauty. But mostly, "Amor Est Mortis" struck me personally with a familiar whisper that clambered back from my past. Softly and sharply, the song plucked out a memory of mine, an uncanny reminder of the words one particular girl had spoken to me earlier that year. They were the words of a broken woman, someone numbed and indifferent enough to submit to me that, "love is dead." Her words, presented both casually and in resignation, rang in my ears like speech from a foreign tongue when I first heard them. At the time I could not fathom such a notion. I imagine it was because I myself had fallen in love with the one who'd spoken them.

---

2.   Susanne Sundfør, "Amor Est Mortis," *Self-Portrait Original Soundtrack, EP*, Bella Union, 2020, MP3.

The drama of love has always been intimately known by my inner self. That familiar angst, the grand imaginings, the heart pangs, were all imprinted upon me as a boy. I don't think I was ever ignorant of the fact that love, and truth for that matter, existed someplace between order and chaos. Acquisition of the good and the beautiful comes with struggle, with exploration, and with endurance. This frontier is a perilous place to venture into, an unknown territory bridging passion and dedication. So it goes that once a portion of these unencountered wonders have been tasted, the potential rewards supersede the risks. Such treasures are revealed as the penultimate fruits plucked from life's many proverbial trees. The heart's initiation and those inaugural romantic encounters are like any coming-of-age story, moving through phases and stages with narrative arcs of many varieties. Truth is discovered, or disclosed, in shocking and delightful complexions, chronicling the movement from oblivious to cognizant. In the end, the naive one is transformed into a self-aware being who can now more adeptly and adequately navigate existence and its most elusive and desired facet, love. Submerged in this introspection, I embraced the knowledge of life as a journey, with unavoidable highs and lows. However, this internal confrontation was suddenly and entirely moot because high above the hidden nooks of Kebler Pass, in the company of Sundfør's voice, I realized that I too had begun to entertain the possibility of love's death.

PROLEGOMENA

"God is dead," it once was said.
Still, I saw Her beauty in yours.
"Love is dead," a girl once mused to me.
I could see the hurt hidden far beneath the contours.

Aren't we magnificent creatures?
Beautiful in our perfect imperfections.
Artful in our subjective deceptions.

Susceptible to fleeting foolishness
and frightfully broken desire.
Terrified of love,
yet eternally in search of its fire.

But if you'll let me,
I'll prove nothing is dead
so long as we still care to dream.

For new beginnings
start with moments
and moments trickle
like brooks
into streams
that forge rivers
and carve valleys.
Moments that ravish.
Thirst.
Fluster.
Flourish.
Flux.
Flow.
Until the flutter
becomes a pulse.
The pulse
a tide.

LILAC

Chamomile warmth wafts
between the candlelight shafts
as the oak boards creak.
The pen's ink scratches
some futile words.
An invitation to this deliberation.
A convocation for this expiation.

Greetings,
I see you've joined.

We've only just begun, friend.
So stir your aesthetic senses now.
Unwrap, with great care, my Moulin Rouge.

Tragedy for the hedonists.
The amusement of nihilists.
Transcendence for us romantics.

Before the foundation of this world,
there was a song written into our visions.
Perceived in legend and myth,
love was fashioned from the fiery tongs of a divine smith.
The potent smelt wounds, destroys and even kills
with pain and fright.
So too it creates, spawning thrills
both of pleasure and delight.
There's an ache and a faint upon its greeting.
Lessons in its nature come and go, so cruelly fleeting.
Even so, the Ancient of Days
still chose to paint love upon the human gaze.

Let us journey into immortal past
where sweet dispositions of naïveté still last.
To the present where paradoxes blossom. Hope holds fast.
Then at last, to a future where shadowy uncertainties await.
An odyssey of fear and trembling, in perpetuity.
Leaving me, for now, in this unsettling ambiguity.
Does love still linger in this world?

Beneath Mexican skies, cielo.
Let me tell you about summer's inferno,
relieved by succulent, smashed pomegranates,
quickly discarded
after kicking a leather ball about in a Spanish mission yard.
I remember so, so much.
The little ones, the orphans, and the crippled boy
who joined us, a goal scored with his crutch.

Back then, imagination never died.

Thunderheads and rain clouds in Puebla.
White sands on the Gulf.

The friendship of two young boys,
whose dreams melded fantasy and sport,
the companionship of girls to court.
Of glorious feats brought to Anfield.
Or of romantic love yet to be revealed.

Oh, the innocent trials of this youth!
So pleasant and so pure.

A STARFIELD'S ROOF //

The glazed belt of the Milky Way
peers down upon us.
Teetering on the edge of the firmament
just close enough to get an earful
of these foolish, innocent proverbs
rolling across a northern lake.

The heavens bend an ear to hear the "wisdom" of youth.
Fondly they listen and chuckle.
The kids dangle legs over the dockside
as the water ripples and bubbles.
Strewn beneath the starglow speaking grandiosely of love,
they're a fellowship of poets like those from bygone days.
Oblivious to the true wonders and pains
that loom before them.

Memoirs are weightless.

Like kindred spirits and Christopher Robin.

Odes to the unwritten sagas of juvenescence.

Their pages unfold and release golden Aspen blades

that splatter across the clouds in their escape.

Timeless, uncradled. Gone with the wind.

"'Tis better to have loved and lost, than never to have
    loved at all." [3]

'Tis better to have lived and lost, than never to have
    lived at all.

---

3. Alfred Lord Tennyson, In Memoriam (Boston, MA: Knight & Millet, 1901), 35.

Prescience and conscience meet.
In urgency they speak;
recite these elegies.
For posterity's sake.

A pretty pebble for the first.
A sad song for the third.
Letters and lilacs for the second.
And a tale written in tomes for the fourth.

All these juvenile antics of a boy with a crush.
But I saved a ring for the last.

A preamble to union.

Lanterns leaking out light into the austere night.

Wintery gales, strong ales, and your bare body

wound up tight with mine.

Affectionate murmurs, silenced, at the notice -

a flurry of white, crystal crowned specks

setting upon the windowpanes.

Curious visitors. Vying for a glimpse.

Shied away, they melt at the warmth of the fire inside.

We'll create this scene, you and I.

Memories only for us.

In this life and the next.

The imagination builds worlds that never die.

Distant ones live in mine.

Skies sprinkled with stardust.

The synthetic melodies of electronic angels.

Signals, they're calling me home.

The heart builds futures one cannot quantify.

Hopeful ones abide in mine.

Lives intermingled with trust.

The laughter of children beneath painted gables.

I've finally come home.

A child seeks the mystery within reality.
The flowering finitude of unity.
At least in this life.
Where stirring expressions of duality
are not fully undone, but live, a nod to eternity.

Amidst floods of turmoil
and harvests of expectation,
new earth unfolds.
It unbinds and bestows,
accosting those who live
in bondage to nostalgia,
yet wed themselves to unrealized futures.

Such a child, the boy, will journey
in pilgrimage, questing for a future worthy.
Through lowlands and heartaches,
midlands and grave mistakes.
To the highlands where the lakes are filled with
divine grace.

Having dwelt in the silhouette of Hermon,
he'd settled for the fall from its slopes into hell.
Until at last, the peak truly beckoned him
to sanctify and summit the mountaintop

where he'd finally come to dwell.
A man now, still a child at heart,
lying beneath the Cedars of Lebanon
beside the woman he'd prayed for.

Come find me when this daydream ends
and the real one begins.

夢の世界 //

Castle in the sky.

A prophetic sight of you inside my eye.

Tell me of what roots and vines will meld an ancient spark

and shelter dreamy souls up high within some soaring ark.

The hanging forests drift. Gardens of the sky.

A dream, a gift, the portents shift.

A cloudy haven, yours and mine.

Come along for the ride dear one

and journey to a place inside my mind.

Then I'll confide just all those things I hope for us to find.

A bare-naked note rings from the old wooden upright.
The gesture of a song's death at the end of day's sunlight.
Then, with her eyes, she urges me on
    in a glimmer of uncreated light.
"Play another. Play another! Do not condemn love just yet."
A pause. Deliberation and consideration.
    Perhaps this is the final reset.
Trees and canopies creak, swaying in the silence.
Then a nod as I slide a meandering palm down her arm
to charm the keys that wait to sing again.
In imperfect elegance we begin.
A kindling, a stirring, a lucent reverie.
Wandering leads, melodies of thought reconfigured
beneath shrouds of dreary leaves.
Fingers dance together, your knuckles
    hugged between mine.
Bare-naked hands making love on the piano
    beneath the pines.

ATLAS //

All corridors depart the Halcyon days.
But I shall return.
I shall return.

VIOLET

A forecast. I'll write into the night,
until apprehension turns my body's drowsy decay
into the soul's warm delight.
This is when I find a fulfilling feast of bread and wine.
In labor and ponderance beneath the lamp
of God's good light.
Clawing for words. Willing art entirely into being.
Cast upward in prayer, in speaking and in breathing.
Freeing incarnate self from internal bleeding.
Fantasy ushered and escorted towards reality.
     Or vice-reverse.
Satellite imaginary. Mapping full expression.
Years of silence were just momentary.
Meaning is ancillary, a cure for depression.

The soul swings out of a Siberian winter.

Exiting a long depression in a romanticist whirl.

Imagining a life with her. The Russian girl.

Something was in bloom.
The glorious resurrection of a trampled spirit.

The days after youth had been spent marooned
    in monotony.
Encountering her was more than some form of
    divine comedy.
A figure melting into the fissures of purple
    predawn brevity.
Perhaps an anomaly. Perhaps a directive trajectory.
Transparent hints, vestigial fingerprints.
    They play with what I've stored away.
Hidden all beneath winter's depressive frost.
    Pieces of myself, forgotten or lost.
It's been a long while for this heart living in exile.

For the bucolic dreamer,
only a faint fondness flowers.
There was nothing sweeter
than her presence, even for a few hours.

It is an innocent gift,
that which is given in ignorance.
That is, when done unrealized.
Blessing another without intention.
In no need of reciprocity.
Few things are purer.

Maybe miracles are people.
And people dream impossible dreams
catalyzing the possible.
This is just a prequel.

Beyond the vale of seasonal gloom
sprouts tussle and vie to climb up into white cloud plumes.
Here, faith is neither absolute nor obsolete;
it plants and harbors dreams for a restless one's sleep.

A PRAYER //

Give me refuge in a northern hamlet
with a Belgian ale and an Irish ballad.
Give me shelter in an old forest
between creaking oaks and blooming Chloris.

Take me by the wrist along the brookside.
To wander with age until we ripen in the countryside.
Mingling with flesh and spirit.
A journey of bucolic hiraeth.

Gift us with truth and humility,
joy, and luminosity.
So we may breathe holy air's tranquility
into eternity.

A step forward. A step into the present.

I have this journal and I'm not sure how much longer

    I can withhold it.

It is as if our day of concurrence and meeting,

    of encounter. . .

is so distant and incomprehensible.

Like a specter among the celestial bodies,

a vanishing point that never draws any closer.

So many years have drifted by,

still you have not yet arrived.

There's a hunger for a presence

even if I cannot fathom its initiation and advent.

      The eternal dilemma.

      To create or to wait.

I now wonder as I wander if I'm the last of a dying breed.
Of renaissance souls reared in dying chivalry,
    steeped in Christian charity.
Living at the periphery, feeding on the epiphanies of the
    new world and the old creeds.
Exuding the summation of both romanticism and
    humanism.

A descendant of impressionism,
I've taken flight from these novel iterations of procession
    and self-assertion.
Lostfully wandering down the crumbling halls of
    Debussian suites,
I glean the vaults and ossuaries of history for the last
    vestiges of anything sweet.
Before the postmodern murder of art—of truth, beauty,
    innocence and the divine spark.

Timidly awaiting
the expansion of hearts
into unison.

LILITH

She tickles my thoughts
so very often.
Dancing me back to paradise.

The last page of the first chapter will write
nocturnally, animatedly, profusely of you and I.
From first encounter to our final goodbye.
Until the ink in the pen falters and finally dries.

And the thunder rolls outside, while I am restless inside.

The rainfall is filled with such a longing.

Do you feel as I do?

Seeking, reaching

for something, someone?

A communion of mystics we are.

Not aimless, not vain,

but sacred beings, aching for the rain.

I don't think...I don't know if God makes plans.

His calendar must be a dance.

With little on schedule, only Love's agenda to advance.

A smile, a fistful of roots.

Do you not know that the divine too can be rueful?!

Hands dirtied, He shakes His head and grins and plants.

His heart is seeding not fate, but chance.

My sycamore is placed beside the foundations
    and a garden bed.

I just hope He finds my tree a home to stead.

Ask what is centered.

What is the center of concrete and abstract things?

Can there be a missing link, strings

abridging mossy knolls and bell towers.

Cedars tower like steeples. God's in the forest.

Church in the old woods.

Pristine and pure, serene and sure.

There it is, the earthen thrum. Harken to its words.

Return me, as an object of my Maker

to a sprawling slumber

where the valleys are carved by glaciers.

There-where I can walk in silence.

At least the kind of silence that removes clutter and noise.

A release from the cacophony of urban distraction and

the briars of orderless, innumerable choice.

Going to the Sun.

On this road I am reborn, born from above.

Now I hear the mourning dove.

The rush of a river's snowmelt.

The ambling deer grunts.

A rustle in the brush. The flight of a thrush.

A turbulent mind divides the chatter from the

unremembrandt. Some cleansing kenosis.

Constant movement to panoptic stillness.

A time to live. A time to self-die.
To halt a thousand-thousand queries and whys.

Contemplative, I trace the outline of a lake's mirror,
embracing the divine face.
I feel time's slippage, its sudden, slowed pace.
Here is the courtyard of the heart.
A place to create. To signify.
The universal dominion of art.
Eternal forms hardly exist so haphazardly,
as ephemeral, vaporious, carnal constructs
or culture's reductionary, profane aqueduct.
no. No. No!
The word is not for the sake of the word,
but for the world beyond the world's words.
Splintered at our glance, the surface is shallow.
Though in the depth below form and sign dance,
dually tied with transcendent cords.
Yes, 'a rose is a rose is a rose.' Its function is not hollow.

Augmented, word and seed are bound and tethered
to a cosmic wind.
To love, to trust, to speak, to believe. All take faith.
The truth behind the shadows in the cave.
There are many leaps that must be entered into and
journeyed until life's end.

Chills are a divine encounter.

A meeting place of spiritual and material.

Gestures from the transcendent.

I don't need to be understood by the world.
Just by one special girl.

Perhaps though, the gripping, fearful truth is
that you'll never truly know anyone, let alone someone.
Perpetually, you'll be confounded.
By the expanse of their mystery.
The shadow of unknowability.

Therein lies the beauty of otherness.
Do not erase this perplexity.
It is an impossible possibility.
Rather, spend an eternity
gazing face to face
hopelessly lost in the new beauties
discovered in each moment.

The author of love is not the self.
It is the *other* and the other Great Other.

Snowmelt and chalets in January.
A serendipitous intertwining
of skis and chemistry.
The pages of Tolkien in your grasp
beneath rivers of dark hair shining.
A portrait of Audrey Tautou.

I often puzzled over it.
For who knows
the reasons
why my heart said no.

Golden for just a moment, but oh so fragile.
Perhaps the first is always a gamble.
At least for most.

Call it primavera.
An Arcadian breeze.
Youthful "acuity."
To be so quickly absorbed into one another.
Anchoring hearts prematurely.

Unaware, that logic is not love
and love is not logical.
I am sorry I had to learn with you
and you with me.

Introspection is a boon.
Caution is wise.
But it's always second guessing.
It plays with moments,
parsing them out
like raindrops on the ground.
Coalescing, conflating,
doubting, and negating.

So, I cringe at my ineloquent words,
spoken hastily.
Because an introvert
has not
the luxury of silence
or a pen to speak.

Truthfully
I'd rather be brief
in my speech.
Then I may marvel
at the ease
with which you
put sound
to thought.
Silencing the mind and
my inner Socrates.

Learning still.
I'm inclined to believe
that love can ebb and flow
like the tides and seas.
One must accept
that you may not always feel
a fierce and roaring flame,
a passion unbound and untamed.
At times it might burn
more like a soft candle.
And at others, a passion so unbridled,
one can barely handle.

Thus, regarding love
I mean not to speak
pretentiously
in universal absolutes
but slowly
in dialectics.
Tempered by inexperience,
wisened by silence
and the quiet insight of divine guidance.

Sometimes mistaken.
Sometimes misunderstood.
Seeking the other's intentions.
Living within the tension of life's questions.

Antiquated attire adorns her.
But she's no relic of the past.
An old soul perhaps.
With only youth in her eyes
and in her grin.

Heirlooms dwell in her heart.
Tethering present, past.
Unwelcome guests perhaps.
Haunting her, they whisper lies,
that beneath the skin, nothing worthy resides.

So she floods life with industry,
knowing that one day
she'll be healed enough to finally flee
to the shores of Sicily.

At last, she ends her litany.
Time to unravel all those dreams
beside the waves of the Ionian Sea.
To rebuild her citadel.
Once cloaked in a winged masquerade
soaked with sacred tears that only God understood.

Now she shines like a beacon.
A lighthouse in the night.
Calling home the man
she'd prayed for since girlhood.

Wake, oh sleeper!
When your daydream ends, our true one shall begin.

A HOPEFUL TRANSMISSION //

Pearls of insight
come to me
in late night reveries.

Perhaps God is a poet too.
And She sees
the purity of my love.

VENUS

Courtship is friend and foe.
The graveyard and garden of the soul.
This is a love letter to the future unknown.
The boulevard of betrothal not betrayal.
Beloved, there is a home.
There is a home.

When you bite your lip,
a funny feeling
bites me.

I can't tame nor rewrite the pages that have already
    turned and faded from the light,
nor erase the persistent power of your feathered scars
    and their sovereign might.
But with each simple slumber and idle day that passes
maybe, just maybe we could trample to ashes
the cold granite walls of impenetrable serenity.

With lofty ambition and renegade devotion,
hope can be reborn in our fleshly vessels
of virtuous emotion.
Every vain and lovesick thought to be devoured,
eternally vanquished, these tattered synapses
freshly empowered.

Why should we not hold onto hope
for something green to return?
For good to reemerge?

Ma chérie, spring is worth the wait.
Coax out your heart,
no longer must it hibernate.

ÉPRIS //

You're amusing
and a muse
to me.

All I really want
is for you
to own my attentiveness,
my tenderness.

To wrap you up in the kindest sweetness.
With the softest kisses.
Fulfilling all your wishes.

To nourish you with waters that heal
and wash away any fear or reserve to feel.

EVERPRESENCE //

Please traverse the chambers of my heart.
Just once.
You'll never leave.

IMPLICIT SOLICITY //

If you could taste my heart,
you'd get drunk
on the ripples
of my adoration.

Saint of my nocturnes.

Chapel of dreams and doctrines.

Question love, but not in Augustinian angst.

Perfect pleasures scare a Stoic's domain.

Pleasure perfects a purified pain.

Do not flee. Do not abstain.

Love is no game. Life is not vain.

Don't meet me with a kiss.
Meet me in a place
of starlight and imagination.
Where touch is slow
and words are sparse.
But the music guides us
to clutched hands…and whispers
that murmur slowly.
Reminding us to bask in this a little longer
before the passionate embrace
of naked, tangled bodies.

Every stroke and every caress.
Every touch and every kiss.
Exists to express
something beyond mere desire.
Let it be absolute affection.
For your sake before mine.
Not my satisfaction but thine.

It's true. C'est vrai.
Waiting is not for-forever.
Maybe forever is for you.

The future is on hiatus and in a mist.
This twilight is terrifying, but it'll desist.

Your past is for dusty shelves and old film reels.
Now, I want you to heal.

What is inscribed upon the inner sanctuary of our souls?

Chaos or calm?
A closed heart or an open palm?
Love takes risk.
Risk takes hope.

Is it beyond my resiliency's scope?
To ascend another woman's slope?

When shall I wade no longer in the shoals?

An evergreen crop top and delicately bared arms
greeted me in feminine mystique.
Dark hair, sharp jaws, white lies.
A petite erudite with nervous energy; a Sicilian physique.
Pale skin, quick speech, emerald eyes.

Nudging brows, I kissed the lids of her closed eyes.
And nearly saw those colossal walls meet their demise.

But gentle touch and caress cannot redress
a being whose heart has been dispossessed.

"Love is dead," she murmured, her hand on my chest.
    "Love is dead."

I wonder if these anxieties are trivial or perilous.
Perhaps a bit of both.

Presently, it has become painfully clear
that to write is hard.

It is clearer that 'tis even harder (for two) to fall in love.

Concomitance is neither coincidence nor construction.
But something in between.

Out of confusion,
mistrust arises.

Out of loneliness,
lust tantalizes.

It is not love! *This*. This is not love.
My heart pleads.

Why did you have to hurt me so?

Time is no constraint.
Or is it?
Patience means restraint.
But must it?

Why are we so afraid
to say what our minds and lips conceal?
To reveal in totality, how we feel?

All these mechanics, the delays, plays and masquerades
are the impermanent whims seeded between the fading
modern day and this new age.
It is but a game.

Surely these highs and lows
mustn't go on forever?

"You're a good man."
She said in earnest.
But there was no salvatory plan.
She just wanted to feel something.
The negation impulse. A gnostic heart convulsing.
    Closing its wings.

I was boy, the collateral romantic. Eternally Hopeful.
    And I loved her.
But nice boys are toys for broken girls hurt by weak men
    and their sinister elixirs.
Tropes aren't cliché when they're lived in.

In retrospect,
there's no ill will
towards the first one to *truly* give my heart a thrill.

I passed your empty building
a year and some months later.
No heart pangs but felt something faded.
Like the low burning sun, my spirit felt ancient
and these bones jaded.

A hazy day drive, down and around through uptown.
The summer city skyline silhouetted
behind power and train lines.
Quiet streets mask crowded rooftop cocktail parties
hidden above cascades of concrete vines.
Down below, a frame from Miyazaki.
A girl on a bike stopped at the tracks.
Silent Love whispers softly in my car, as I stall at the light
and watch from afar.
Just someone new, with an echo of your skin,
your spirit's Mediterranean hue.
This grainy film is a daydream or a requiem
and she isn't you.

Somewhere far off, a church bell rings,
calling the faithful to mass.

But here I am, an apostate for the day, seeking a pint,

a wine, or some small, vapid glass.

To live a little, to heal a lot—not to outwit the cosmic clock

or dim or refract the past.

Gazing off into the sun daze, she waited for me to pass.

I lurched forward and put my foot to the gas,

letting fugitive memories leave in peace.

You've departed at last.

Sayonara.

Portraits in waiting.
That is what we are.

A tortuous evolution
of canvas after canvas.
Discarded, one then another.
Like templates which are
reused and forgotten,
erased and restarted.

Coaxed from the cocoon
before the time was ripe.
Forced to make the crooked straight,
to divide wrong from right,
on our own.

We're a long way from home.

Summer departed with a sigh.

A mingled inferno, stricken into slumber.

The earth on fire, perdition's haze rising higher.

A dearth of meaning.

Wasted lands, the city gnaws the lumber,

cursing the bucolic hand that feedeth,

heaping shame upon the simpleton, the outdated ways.

Is there no escape? No golden age, no heavenly gaze?

"Adapt and change," they say,

"The seasons are temporal. Nothing is eternal,

save death, taxes, and infinite reversal."

There's a hole in our world's soul.

A leakage in mine that I can't control.

What can make it whole?

LILY

November rain drains
the chlorophyll from leafy veins and membranes.
A herald. Autumn will be gone soon.
Stressing, stretching me,
it suggests that the years are too swift
life too arbitrary, to pass on love's indiscriminate gift.
To wait and wait and wait
for it to manifest of its own accord,
or of some divine reward.

This modern template is tired and void.
An impression of aimless humans
grasping at existential straws.
Determined to govern our nature,
abnegating admittance to its fatal flaws.

Another round, another night of gunshots
skipping by my windows.
Strange how close death is. Its space from life is liminal.
Haphazard Earth. A murderous intent in every hurl.
Its mighty blights, thunderbolts, even its people.
Bullets kill the flesh, yes, and heartbreak the spirit.
Oh, what a world.

I'm a wild child. Cannot be quelled, cannot be felled.
My heart runs free.
I don't know how not to feel this strongly.
That Celtic soul in me, it rears its mythic visage
of refulgent bounty
when it hears those sorrowful Uilleann pipes
in the highlands across the pond.
Then I believe, others still understand
the terrible beauty and tragedy
of love and heartbreak.

Do *you* ever hear that note or two at the onset of a song?
A wind, a word, the old longing.
They shatter and shiver.
Piercing so sharply.
There, there it is. A heart pang. A gut punch of belonging.
Then you think.
That, *that* hurts.
God. Why do I have to feel *so* much?
A flood of relived moments.
Aches and nostalgic currents.
Elysian yearning.
Lost dreams returning.

I don't know how to escape this melancholy.
So much provokes this internal privation.

Am I simply yoked to feelings for another high,
 another rush?
In anticipation of the possible touch of another
 heart's brush?

Do I love what I cannot have
    for love's sake?
Or am I chasing what
    I cannot grasp
precisely because
    of its elusiveness?

Viridity, isn't it?

No.

I think not.

I've always worn this heart on my sleeve.

One ventures the unknown so two may cleave.

There is little to hide.

Passion and choice must always coincide.

Love is a feeling.
A flicker and a whisper.
An unraveling, like a river.
Moon dances, an impulse to kiss her.

Selah.

But love too is a choice.
A vow, something beyond the inner voice.
While you must always have one,
'tis infinitely preferable
to have both.
For when one fades
then the other remains.

CORNERSTONE //

Love is not merely the byproduct of chance
or happenstance.
It must be built.
Build with me darling.
Construire avec moi.

I want heart insurance.

But perhaps I need heart *assurance*.

Maybe that's what I'll call it.

To be greeted by horizons of longing in your gaze.

To write a novel, not a chapter, not a passing phrase.

But how does one attain it?

Are you a Trojan horse?

Should I close my gates?

Seal my letters?

Or fling them wide

without delay or hesitation?

L'amour est terrifiant.

I don't want to scare you off.

I want to show you something

you've never seen before.

Shall I open the floodgates?

Oui ou non?

Oh, the places we'd go.

Oh, the things we'd do.

Learn Français together. Parlez-vous?

Take a Haitian rendezvous.

Lagoon in the Caribbean blue of Port Salut.

Migrate again, marry and merge our bodies in Toulouse.

Disrobe, tarry and overstay our welcome.

Unfold, sow love, grow old and peruse

with each other.

I'll peer into a soul
and find home for my own.
A perfect fit. A perfect nook.
Two lover's nest beside God's brook.

Follow the evolution.
The decreation of indissoluble resolutions.
Through word and touch as I fall and clutch.
Perhaps you'll see how I tussle with romance
or shake my fist at faith,
dealing with coincidence and chance.

Regarding deeds or charity, given or received,
emotional affairs enclosed in short-lived revelry,
I could write and write.
There's some distance between fleshly chemicals
   and the spiritual elementals.
Still, surely there is a kind of desire that is pure,
   not remotely touched by any evils.

Realize that I've kissed and kissed only one.
The burden of mine now
is the want and the risk
to kiss and kiss
only one more.
Once more.

VAPOR

I am a sleeping forest.
You stumble beneath my canopies
and my branches will catch you.

I am a wandering brook.
In my waters you'll find no pretenses.
When I love, I'll lay aside my dams and defenses.

When I've dared to let it in again,
it's nice to feel that flutter
in my heart
once more.
To get high
on just a thought
for just a moment.

Reminded though
to reel it in
with caution and with care.
But still
in hope and expectation.
So a moment can become
a series of frames
strung together
like polaroids on the wall.

Hung there
not for one season
but for many.

She is classy.
Exuding femininity and poise.
The sun's kiss upon her skin, a warm caress.
A girl with European soul.
Unafraid to frolic barefoot, for an evening stroll,
in her white dress.

Everything about her makes me weak.
Yet somehow, I'm not a fool in her presence.
What a wondrous miracle this is!

There are echoes of beautiful lives lived all around us.
Archived in blurry photographs of black and white.
I want to capture all of yours.

You are so safe with me
beautiful lady.
Let your heart roam my steppes
as you wander my address.
You are my guest.
I'll be your guide.
Beside you step and stride.

You keep playing my heartstrings
faster, louder, stronger.
You may be,
the sweetest melody
that's ever danced through
the caverns of my heart.

I've so much to show you,
little sparrow.

A world of cosmic islands
far from the city.
Tucked back in those sleepy hollows
which are so dreamy and laconic.
They sit beneath harmonic horizons
awaiting us in their unperturbed silence.

I've so much to show you.

Misty mornings on northern lakes.
Where we'll dance and waltz in ice skates
under hidden pine boughs
and freshly fallen snowflakes.

I've so much to show you.

Shimmering silver screens
and delicate movie scenes.

And finally, tenderness.
Yes, my complete tenderness.

Dove-like kisses on your neck.

An evening beside candles, a raincheck.

My fingers behind your ears

twirling your storm soaked hair.

Whispering with their touch

I will help quell your fears.

Soften the memory of those tears.

I've so much to give you.

I'd carry you to Verona.

If you'd let me.

Your dreams are mine.

Pacing through the garden, I thought to myself;
Maybe she'll find beauty in the pieces of me that I don't.
Maybe she'll teach me to love the parts of me that I won't.

I wander and I wonder beneath this windowed sky.
Does love winter and wither like all green things
beneath the sun, only to die?

I see flora and fauna.
Tangled pasts and repeated trauma.
Jasmine and Magnolia.
Divergent futures, with one bereft of drama.

Endlessly, the paths of speculation and truth duel and spar,
but also intersect and guide you like the north star.

One can only hope that those words and moments
mean as much for you as they do for me.

'Alas, love and war is cyclonic.
And misplaced hope, a bittersweet tonic.

‏מִילְבֶה לְבָה‎ //

I don't just fall in love with a girl.
I fall in love with her name.
With her family.
Her pensive gaze.
Dark wisps in the wind,
the color of her hair.
The tight press
of her dress
against the small
of her back.
Smitten by that fleeting touch
and her undressed wrists.

Do I truly perceive her form? It shifts and wavers.
Is this true essence or smoke, mirrors, and vapor?
Where is the virgin land beyond infatuation
and one-sided labor!

I don't just fall in love with a girl.
Aura, myth, or the real. It matters little.
I let her take my heart for a twirl,
watching as she turns such aspirations to hevel.

The passions of the heart. . .

Shall we mitigate? Moderate?

Or will self-control merely exasperate.

Turning presence into absence.

Like grains of shifting sand vanishing from the crest
of a desert dune.

On a windless, starry night. Beneath a godlessly silent
and impassible moon.

DEMURE DISCORD //

I adore the pieces you've given me.
But I know there's so much more of yourself
hidden behind the seawall.

You scaled my outer ramparts,
so I'll let you in.
Even if you can't do the same.

But are there cracks in your walls?
Or are you just another her? The false fall.

Broken is beautiful.
Broken is also hurtful.

Hands layered, laid across another,
    we skipped, one after the other
over a bridge-puddle just below the falls and
    the hanging vines.
Up a stone staircase we raced, then caught our breath
    and embraced, beneath the tall pines.
A reluctantly long hug, now it's all annulled.
I the cautious one,
you the weaver of a strangely urgent thread.

THE ORCHARD //

Oaken umbrellas shield the soft sun in its distant equinox.
But splinters and shards dart through leaves,
reminders of this year's turning clock.
Some ways up a dirt road, surrounded by a pine grove,
    I sit with my sister.
She consoles my confusion. "Life," she says,
    "is not *only* a trickster."

The contents of her mind's cistern nurture,
    like the flow of a spring river.
Gifting patience and appeasement
to my body's inner quiver.

I always hoped to fall in love in the fall,
amidst autumn leaves.
But for now, I suppose I'll have to wait,
beneath the molting of an orchard's eaves.

Revenant. Don't leave me with your revenant.

Covenant. Join me with a covenant.

Or flee my memory for eternity.

Complete absence or total presence.

"When my heart is ready—I hope you'll wait for me.
I'll come back—if you hold tight this guarantee."

Exit Tiamat.
Enter Marduk.
Three Months. An excursus.
Giving *him* a third, a fourth, a fifth shot.
She returns. An afterthought.
A heart rebuked.

It will pass.

But right now, I can't undertake a single damn task.

My body aches.

My mind quakes.

I can't complete the art I must.

Can't bridge the gap

between mind and matter, thought and word,

desire and deed.

Indeed, when I look into the future,

    I see only vain ambition, struggles, and gasps.

When I peer into the past, I catch only vapor,

    soon dispatched from my grasp.

Each day, under an ancient sun

another heart is undone.

"I love the way your eyes give me your attention."
The compliments sat with me, gnawing the psyche.
Weighing me down until there was enough to sink
my pneuma into the earth.
But at the gates I stopped and turned away,
with new awareness, enough to quickly flee Hades.
My gaze was satisfaction for an appetite;
egoism's extension.
After all, we are only the sum of our neuronic cravings.
Survival of the indifferent.

Exhausted. Haunted. Taunted.

By the games people play.

The hearts cruel ones slay

without dismay.

Another one, another day.

Bonded together with intimate words you can't unsay.

Fool's play, with adornments of pleasure and indulgence,

a piquant taste of mental foreplay.

Romance temporarily flaunted and cast away,

another conquest to display.

But she's only a tease and you—well—

    now a withered bouquet.

The art of cat and mouse, of love and prey.

Here in the morning and gone by midday.

Well.
A circle complete.
She's done what I'd feared.
"I won't do what she did to you."
MY God! I even begged for *you* to spare me.
But affectations. Those bloody feelings.
They just can't be mitigated.

Numb.
Is there nothing left to feel?
Hushed despair
is all.
It's a small consolation, I suppose
to be unable even to cry.

I despair because I care.
I despair because life seems arbitrary, cruel, and unfair.
Maybe I need more humor.
Comic relief? That'll expel me from this stupor!
"Life's a cosmic joke. We're just Darwinian beings
governed by materialism!"
Says the militant skeptic.
Well, I say materialism fucking sucks.

Was that poetry, or one of my tangents?
No idea.

Tell.
What's the point of falling anymore?
You reveal how you feel, and you lose.

Hope has died.
Love may too.

You whispered sweet somethings
that meant little to you and so much to me.

This deception awakened a rage I've never known.
An anger that suffocates my softness.
A hurt embittered by your callousness.

If love is dead, so is God.
If God is dead, so is love.
We'd murder them both
and call it transcendence.
Some fools we are.

FALSE REIFICATION //

A phantom haunts my heart.
She has a name.

A ghost walks upon the earth.
She returned to woo me.
But I wouldn't play her game.

ANTILEGOMENA

I stumbled amidst your roots,
awakening a tormentor of souls.
Do I speak too harshly?
To move swiftly from infatuation to adoration.
To end in cessation and fomentation.
It was primal. It is terminal.
These incidental sentiments and
conventional standards declared
that blind faith overruled the capacities of pure reason.
For the causes to love can be adequately few
and still filled with internal treason.
Feelings are not infallible!
Your truth…is never unimpeachable.
Am I not a victim of my own aesthetic bifurcation?
A merchant of penchant flirtation?
As an ornate veneer tells only the story it desires,
hiding deadly passions and fires
of destruction and iniquity.

The chaotic whims of those living past modernity.
Vindicated, I'm untangled now from the patterns
evident in such a destructive prowl.
Was it a mirage of faith or of faculty?
Prayers unrequited, ignored in order to protect me?
Disenchanted now but not destroyed.
Delivered before the essential me turnt null and void.
Hobbling along, I live.
Mostly vicariously. In poems and films.
Still playing out cosmogonic dreams
that I'll find something true.
The love of my life. Pure romance's birth.
See, I know now with conviction, my own infinite worth.
Belle femme, your arctic empire will melt.
Thawed by the gales of an ocean
which you'll sink into;
the primordial chaos of self-love.
Deeper still, into the grottos of the
hollowed earth you've created.
Where you'll revel beside the pools of
alchemy and ancestral wickedness.
A reflection of Narcissus.
Collapsing in upon yourself.
Crucifying all who dared love you.

External beauty is fleeting.
But the trajectory of the heart echoes into eternity.
Au revoir.

When Truth fades,
only power remains.

The world has changed, forever.

沈黙 //

The absence of God is felt in my essential being.
The silence of His spirit is defiantly deafening.
Could nothingness be a sound of its own,
or a signal from the marrow that doubt is sewn
to skin and bone?

Home is the spiritual.
Earth not purely material.
Thrust into some world through some providence,
we wrestle with angels and demons as we strive for survival.
There seems often to be no arrival
as truth escapes its rivals.
But Truth exists. It must persist.
Polarity. Attraction. Mechanics. Thermodynamics.
Law is the Letter of the Universe.
Eternal. Divine. Human. Natural.
Love is the letter of the Law.
The Center of it All.

Innocence and instinct.

Impulse and insight.

Creatures of habit. Citizens of earthen havoc.

Timid and rabid. Dramatic and erratic.

We evolve. We devolve.

Increasingly lavish, progressively savage.

The sheltered, the "enlightened,"

    all inhabit the same passage.

Both wed to the pendulum,

    they each carry their own baggage.

Ruminations and contingencies.

Realizations and epiphanies.

Resuscitations and hostilities.

Many doors have shut.

So I'll add another.

For it is not in my essence to be bitter.

I'll not let the sun set on this anger.

Healing is coming swifter.

But I must wonder one final time.

Was I merely a timely token?

A hidden rose to pluck.

A pleasant reminder of the fish in the sea?

Did you ever truly give a fuck?

I was *Athelas*.

Kingsfoil for what he did.

The love of mine simply wasn't the highest bid.

You wrote poems for me

and I for you.

But I suppose that was your cathartic healing.

Oh, well wasn't that freeing.

Yes, I see now how these words are birthed in irony.

Down beneath the poplar grove, a leaf or two settled
    upon my journal.
Far from the canopies of life they've strayed.
I recall how the violence, brokenness, and disarray
of humanity can be undone.
For love, not death, is the great equalizer.
Perhaps Dostoevsky was no idealist.
Yes, beauty confounds. It riddles too.
It leaves me hoping this at least is somehow true.
That, "Beauty will save the world." [4]
Beauty in all its aesthetics…
its aspirations,
sensations and creations,
becomes inevitable.
Unyielding in conviction.
Beauty *shall* save the world!
The nihilist will not utter the last word.
The spokes of evil
will slow and shrivel
with every act of kindness, tenderness, and forgiveness.
No matter how simple or small.
That is the beckoning of God's true mandate and call.

I tuck a leaf between wordless and empty pages,
    closing my journal.

---

4. Fyodor Dostoevsky, *The Idiot*, trans. Alan Meyers (Oxford: Oxford
   University Press, 2008).

I am a seeker of Truth and of Love.
In all honesty, I don't know where I'll end up.
But somehow I'm certain, that here on earth,
waters of life and love will fill my flesh's drying
    incarnate cup.

Incidental beings.
Somewhat accidental feelings.
These emergent pathways
always seem to guide me to empty walkways.

I've been in love once.
In like plenty.
A cut to the Achilles heel
almost drained me, I'm close to empty.
The bloodletting nearly fatal.
It hurt a great deal.
Mistakes of my own. Been too quick to feel.
A heart touched. A few times crushed.
Never in a rush, so now it's time to heal.

LÚTHIEN

Spring, spring!
Oh faithful spring.
You keep my heart, you build me wings.
You light winter's dark, a fresh new start.
A goddess' death, a garden's new breath.

Spring, spring!
Oh wakeful spring.
Tell me season—what wondrous gifts this year will bring?
Vain insurances, venial assurances.
Unbind the petty burdens and feed this fervent soul
endurance.

Out of her body, Marduk built the cosmos.
Out of your falsity, I'll build what only real love knows.

A little healing
    comes every day.
A new hurting
    comes either way.
It's as if brokenness and rebirth
are eternally simultaneous
    until the closing of the age.

A myriad of learning
    guides me through the fray.
A heart ever shorn of boyhood
    and filled with dismay.
Still filled with radiance,
    waiting until the turning of a new page.

SUFFERANCE //

I'm still so…tired of opening up
to those who take the beauty inside for granted.

And a great fear persists, insists
that I'm simply unable to describe the depth of my soul.
Its love for lost moments of beauty.
For grandeur and for wonder,
its nostalgic murmurs.
Its transcendentalist ramblings.

But I still believe that tenderness
is the telos of life
and the panacea for strife.

There is a deity.
For only a fool declares in their heart
that there is no God.
But divine orchestration, there is not.
No architecture to life's meanderings.
No determinative structure to a heart's sundering.

Only voices and choirs
directing souls with lyres
to the schematics of liars.

This is no assault on tradition.
Nay, let us make war against subjective subjection and
spiritual narcissism.

There are choices and misguided desires.
Proven courses and uncharted waters.
And those who tie cowardly decisions
to heavenly revelations.

Late night earnesty.
I'm caught in a reverie.
Its beauty scares me.
The way it echoes her in everything.
There are residuals I must erase,
patterns to trace and face.

Is it repetition or fulfillment?
Alchemy or true love's advent?

Forgiveness is the entrance,
the pathway to invite a new presence.
The singular bride.
But first I must dispense with my pride,
jettisoning all those poisonous momentos
in pursuit of a pure heart, guided through new meadows.
This doorway is opened, but not of my own will.
Only the Teacher can guide the student up that hill.

So, Christ-Logos, incarnate man.
True-born of Woman. Second Adam.
The mystery of the divine intertwined with mine.
The task of forgiveness for her is now thine.

Mellow or dramatic?
I am both.
Frantic or fanatic?
I am not.

A boy loses himself when subsumed.
When he forgets his native dreams and substitutes.

The written speech conveys
an essence that the reader determines in their mind.
But beyond that, lies the intention
and that has its own kind.
What is made of this all, I leave for you to decide.

Is it not a sighing epigraph?
A display of moments in time, "Lost, like…tears in rain."[5]
A man penning a literary photograph.

---

5. *Blade Runner.* Directed by Ridley Scott. Burbank, CA: Warner Bros
Studio, 1982.

We live under the shadowy impression
that healing or celebration
is merely a matter of putting into comprehension
things better left to contemplation
or un-explanation.
Ignoring the power of leaving some things unspoken.

For certain joys and pains cannot be grasped with speech.
And the eternal desire to do so
annihilates the mystical beauty and sorrow
of the human experience.

We must relearn the art of silence.

But this season of silence
is a watermark, a lingering of the things you'd given me.
It feels like violence.
Your indigo raindrops tattoo my conscience,
coloring all I see.

The heart steals.
The heat feels.
The heart heals.
The heart keels
over and takes
all that life deals.

A notice to whom it may concern.
My heart is closed for the season.
Or should I say, on hold.
I'm feeling just a bit too cold.
Maybe I'll fly to Belfast
to wait out this winter, until its gales have passed.
Until this time of healing reaches its threshold.

Either way, I'll be eagerly awaiting the eve of spring.
For there in the ground, I believe someone will find
seeds already planted, accrued, and ready to sing.
Flowers to bloom.
Into cerulean blue, purple and all hues.
Coriander or Saffron, Laurel or Valerian,
Aster and Marigold.
Corral them all and find a vase.
Then quite a story will be told.

Spring now.
I'd anticipated your departure
from the interior of my lost paradise
for some time.

But it supplanted my supple garden
inserting Pandæmonium in its stead.

Not sure when or if
forgiveness came forth
when I let you go.
But more was lost than just you.

Schweitzer spoke truest,
"The tragedy of life is what dies inside a man
while he lives."[6]

That is the legacy of this heartbreak.
A man set adrift and aloof.

Surely despair is the fount of creativity,
the wellspring for resurgent artistry.

Wait for summer's eve.
For the acacia and the cedar to green.
Then a wilting heart will finally be seen.

---

6. This quote has been attributed to both the German theologian and
   philanthropist, Albert Schweitzer and the American journalist
   Norman Cousins.

A gift of kalopsia this greying morning
as we settle in for the long winter.
The heart in hibernation
will unearth a spring reincarnation.

By mistake
I encountered your memory
in a stray photograph.

Those dreams, set aside
so that others may reside.
Then, in time
both will coincide and thrive.

Loss is only consoled and conciliated when confronted.

The thawing indulges room for flowers
where frozen ground once reigned.

SEAFLOWER //

Shades of oceanic
synthwaves remind me
that dreams never die,
they're just forgotten
or temporally surrendered.
Like faint melodies
that stubbornly refuse to fade.
Like prodigal memories that never quite age.
Once cherished. Somehow lost.
Soon to be found once more.

ΔΙΚΑΙΟΣύνη //

I was told that it was Sappho who once said,

'Justice is when the one you love, loves you back.'[7]

That sounds like justice to me.

I want that kind of justice.

---

7. This is a paraphrase from a lecture given by Professor David Fredrickson of Luther Theological Seminary. It echoes a poetic motif found in the works of the Greek poet Sappho of Lesbos (circa 630-570 BC), which can be traced centuries afterward. For further discussion of this motif, see David E. Fredrickson, *Eros and the Christ: Longing and Envy in Paul's Christology* (Minneapolis, MN: Fortress Press, 2013).

CORAZÓN TONTO //

A little particular.
A bit too over-eager.
A little young.
A bit too heartstrung.

Yes, I was always the hopeless romantic.
The boy writing songs for girls
with dark hair and pretty names.
Now I'm not so sure that I can keep falling
so hard and so fast.
Pierced with shards of disappointment
I find there's resentment now.
And I resent that I can't trust the way I used to.
Call it the hollowing of naïveté.
A shattering of adolescent sanctity and purity.

Embedded deep down remains a remnant
I hope to guard and keep.
Still, I'm afraid that portions and pieces
are beyond recovery.
Shipwreckt, without prospect of any rediscovery.

And I'm just not sure I want to chase another.
Why must I take the greater leap and risk the greater fall?
Let go, you say?

Mmm…

It's a proposition

I just can't answer yet.

Maybe I'll let someone chase me…

It just seems we never want the same people.

Someone always beckons to a more alluring call.

Someone always cares a little more…or, a little less.

Don't bother meeting halfway.

I know because…halfway does not exist.

I suppose it's the human condition.

Nevertheless I ask…

When will I pluck my violet?

A vintage midnight—developments in latency.
Putting an incandescent light
to countless unwritten vacancies.
Cordoned off within the parameters of my room.
This pen at last begins to dry.

Settled in spirit,
I found myself for once
under the spell of no particular woman.

Perhaps this is freedom.
Perhaps it's indifference.
Perhaps it's healing.
Or maybe I've reached a point of resurgence.
Finally finding some meaning in immanence.

Dusk's sun—cloud lines running like a time lapse
are eroding the walls of age, unwinding the gaps.
Tonight,
I felt like that boy again.
Treading the fields of grass and green,
rehearsals of happy days that had been.
Pleasant souvenirs from the stomping grounds
which taught me how to fall without qualms.
What was once a fragmented capacity is opened
at the gate of the Psalms.
An invocation, an exhortation to my spirit—ending
the diaspora—the dissensus.
Like an archaeologist, I've dug up artifacts
from my renaissance.
The butterflies have returned.
The flowers' growth is relearned.
The immensity of evocation and sensuality now churns.
Today,
a new happiness is draped on this evening's sun.
A fresh wind fills once breathless lungs.

ECLOGUE //

Mithlond in the west
is where my heart and mind used to quest.
Or the shores of Amroth in the south,
which harken to our world and its Thracian seas.
In the shaded glades of old growth forests, awaits the past.
This, yes this, is where my future holds it keys.
The place of stone bridges, cottages, ferns and fertile fields.
A world before industry and moral apathy
revealed their failing yields.

On a new shelf I'll save those tales,
some homespun readings for my daughters.
Between garden and grave, those fables their life will pave.
Passing on a potter's clay to write with delight
    timeless dreams that'll stay.
A legacy deferred, stirred and transferred from their
    father's younger days.

I feel it again—that readiness to love.

It arrived with the warmth and the end of winter's spell.

And I see how capable, how vast is this well

with its empyrean capacity.

Truly how much *one* woman will draw from it

once I allow the heart of hers to dip

into the borders, the hearth of mine.

How strange it is.
I thought so minimally of you at first light.
For a long year,
until we met last night.
Our first sight.

You lean in.
A tilt and a dip of your head as you listen with intent.
A careful and attentive spirit. At ease and content.
Your little left arm tucks the cropped dark hair behind
  your ear.
It rests there. Elbow creased and rested upon the
  tabled tier.

Oh, sweet heaven on earth! Why do you tease me,
with something that I'm not sure is meant to be?
She's an angel.
There's harmony in my heart. Already at the start.

Shall I leap? Shall I leap? Shall I leap?
She's just a girl. Just a girl. Just a girl?

Why then does her image walk before my eyes?
With me each moment beneath heaven's skies.

That is the desire I waited upon and hoped to return.
I second guess myself, but recall that love's design is for
a heart to truly burn.
Is that reckless, roiling longing within you too?

Our paths will cross. Then let us see where it takes us two.

Dwelt in an eternal moment in my mind.
Awash in the sea flow,
your presence shimmers on the waters.
Divinely designed, pastorally inclined.
Immersive in its radial patterns.
Unmet, your aura dashes through lagoons,
catacombs, and caverns.
A summons, sufficient to water my currents and dreams.
My galley departs. Esperanza rises.
Undefined. Somehow refined.
Existent someplace unconfined,
beneath the southern horizon.

Such pretty eyes.
Yours have a mystic guise.
I wonder what they'll see looking into mine.

Do you wonder, in a thousand years,
if a man will still find within him
the wont and the desire, nay the will
to just sit in the sun, to slow down, to watch other beings
as they walk, to and from, down a forested street.
To smile as a little one first finds her feet
or two new lovers again converge and greet.

Will time's march break our essence?
Will our embodied souls dissipate,
self-destructing as we turn to a meaningless existence
hushed by the pace of human progress
and moved to isolation?
A suspension of the beautiful,
rendering the spiritual useless.

We near the end or some old beginning's new wind.
All beauty has its return,
    old melodies their timeless sound.
Love must rend and mend the new age,
    then resurrection shall abound.

In fields of light
in another (kind of) life,
there are pastures to withdraw.
With wonder and with awe.
Their stone fences are borderlands and guardrails.
The woods, the glades,
the parishes, and their restful shade.
An archival escape from life's unceasing descent;
    its abject censure, its performative pace.
An inversion or an end. The cessation of tempests
    and winds driving the unending race.
Falling. Falling. Falling. This is a coupe de grâce.
Not the End of All Things, but a respite and a foretaste.
Merely the death knell of one new order.
The bell tolls, but soon comes another.
Here comes a kiss, the peace of lux æterna.
Its real presence at my feet and in my hands.
Bread of life. Living water. Heaven's manna.

In the flatlands of modernity,
the cathedrals are empty and the graveyards full.
Dead are many living souls,
but the bodies crawl and move and mull.

Branded, we consume and pollute.

Insatiable, there is nothing we will not seek to doom or ruin.

We sell beauty. We gouge it out.

Defacement of nature and the womb,

taking Earth to its tomb.

Commodified. Prosaic. Conformed.

Our art is cynical. Really, 'tis form is deformed.

Art will save the dormant heart.

Accrual not for one's own sake.

For the craft and not the masses.

Expression incarnate, little vignettes in gloss and matte.

Proffered in vindication of oneself before God and a lover.

Impermanence, in exile on the outskirts of Eden

where the substance in the soul-space

will someday return through some organic sluice gate.

Now it waits and creates. The divine it imitates.

An authentic template born of the first mandate.

So restless here in the new West.

How I long to flee this place.

It is not the City of God.

Nor the fertile garden of *adam*.

Its sins are mortal. The daily concerns, feeble and petty.

A melancholic space. The parlours emptied.

Its springs languish and the seekers come away hungry.

No mundo interior. No prime meridian.

It is not God's country.

The margins disintegrate.

An exhaustion. An evaporation.

A loss of vision and intuition.

¡Abierto, abierto! The door is open.

But the house is vacant and formless.

There are no windows.

There are no seas.

Nothing worthy left to see or to believe.

Where is the kingdom, the Kingdom of God?

Not purely within nor purely without.

But on the cross and in the doubt.

LE CYGNE //

Like a swan, you dip and preen
to see what hidden spaces lie behind my shadow screens.
Your body it bends. Your lips seem to quiver.
Yet, all I can feel is the pounding in my heart
as my old dream renews with your whisper.
I want a love that will pound on my door,
asking please to enter!
And yes, I'll open, I'll finally open.
The tears will flow and the years will slow
as we shake and tremble in the harvest; an infinite glow,
    our holy repose.

Testimonies, tests, and trials.
All to beautify someday, the walk down lilac aisles.

Poetic theatrics
compiled to unveil my soul's unwritten secrets.

You forayed into the sea of my blushing internal blue,
all to hear about a boy, a man, who has yet to say,
    "I love you."

There are disparate realms of love.

Some where fantasy and reality collide

Some where hurt and mistrust finally die.

Some which envision a she and I.

SUMIRE //

I tread in her shadow.
Her gaze I hope to eternally borrow.

The prospect is envious.

Slow design through the jealous beat of time.

She and he bond.

Oh they could be fine. So fine.

Staggering through the alleys of endless reality

they've declined a hundred of love's offers,

even potent inquiry.

Sober hearts shuttered and weary, still they may soon

be open and pure and ready.

ASHITAKA & SAN //

Touch the top of my lip with the bottom of yours.
We'll skip and prance, romancing our way through
spring's vernal doors.
Exchanging breath,
our healed lands will hold hands and bloom to life
after winter's long death.

Tales from chapters yet to be.
The emergence—the confluence
Of new habitats; a virtuous concupiscence.
The merging of twin flames.
One sculpture made with two names.
Eden in the valley.
Consummation—passion's first finale.
Dual magnolias wrapped up in perfect *shalom*.
Built with adamantine touch stones that warden our home.
Order and beauty.
Chaos and beast.
A sensual feast
On one another's ardent love.
Harkening from the West to the East.
From sea to sea.
We learn to just be.
The perfect equilibrium—composed and carefree.
A divine orchestration, a symphony.

The sun and its structure is fickle
in the light of your countenance and its prismatic rays.
A refraction, a chimera. Yours disquiets and ruptures me.
As I've come with expectation
through the disappointment of your doorways,
I ask, "What is courtly about love?"
Is it a sacrament or a madness?
It seems a companionless altar.
There is no baptism, no ascent.
No kiss from a rose or God above.
The Lord is not there and the maiden I dream of
is distant and unaware.
The Throne is absent. My visions are scattered.
Trussed and closed, I see the Euphorian gates
are not mine to open or shatter.

The veil is torn, His descent like a dove.
My idle pursuits collapse.
See my child, how little now you yet know of love?
Nakedness. I thought my soul's candor
I could from you have spared.
How I've felt that the Watchmaker had no clothes
until His wrists are turned to embrace me
and the scars are bared.

His admonitions whisper,

and I finally turn to listen, "Yes, Father?"

Overeager I know, but must I set these hopes aside?

At least for now, beloved. Just abide.

Iconoclastic. Cleansed of all idolatry.

Not the crucifix, but of a fancied ring and its potent rivalry.

Find yourself. Find Christ. Then your heart will be ready.

Wherever, whenever, whomever it is,
I just pray our hearts are not consummated
until the right hour.
So we may arrive together upon eternity's shore.
Yes, I do believe new life will one day flower.
Death will part us for a time, yes, but it is merely a door.

"THE SHADOW PROVES THE SUNSHINE"[8] //

My dreams are a seal upon my existence.

An allegiant expression of love's persistence.

A verdant, violinic arpeggio of insistence.

Urging me onward. A life of resistance

to nihilism and all that is untoward, sadistic, and listless.

---

8. Switchfoot, "The Shadow Proves the Sunshine," *Nothing is Sound*, Columbia/Sony BMG, 2005, Compact Disc.

Rest.

Twilight is gathering, dark clouds soon to descend.

Yet new dawns loom.

Rest.

Night is swift, soon to end.

While stars are veiled, unplayed hymns can still bloom.

// BENEDICTION //

May the morning air kiss your lips with its coolness,
the sun your cheeks with its radiance.
May the skies paint your eyes with its colors
and the Lord your heart with His wonders.
May the tears be wiped from your cheeks as you sleep
and your hurts smothered out like torches in the night's deep.
May the moon light your steps with its guidance,
the stars a compass even in their silence.

And may my love lay upon your breasts like violets.
Petals upon your chest fallen like notes from violins
A flood of zealous gifts as we open new wineskins.

EPILEGOMENA

Life's far too fragile and short
to veil the tremors of the heart.
And while I tremble as I write,
only this catharsis can soothe these blights.

I so often speak blithely of my "romantic side."
Upon further reflection, the absurdity of this tenacious
mantra has dawned upon me. Yet, even in spite of my acute
awareness of this penchant, I continue to mindlessly make
use of this phrase as if it were axiomatic to my existence.
Perhaps my thought patterns have been subjected
to the supposed sophistry of Cartesian dualism,
as if reason and feeling or logic and emotion could
ever truly be disentangled from one another.
As if the whole of something could be extracted and
deconstructed piece by piece and left unscathed.

For while parts compose the entirety, the sum
cannot be itself through subtraction.
That is precisely why no single "side"
exists, romantic or otherwise.

Quite the opposite.
You see, my being, my embodied soul, is a
complex array of webs and synapses.
"Well of course!" You say. "We all know this to be true."
But my vantage point insists that it cannot solely be the
firing of neurons that explains the origin *or* the ferocity
of emotion. Surely such phenomena must expand
beyond the realm of observation and explanation.
When every fiber and bone is a pulsating, undying
energy that remains hopelessly and unabashedly
romantic, perhaps then, new methodologies must be
applied to analyze such marvels. Why not abandon
rote formulas for the panacea of sound and melody and
poetry. The questions that ail and beleaguer us all and
the desires that afflict are not resolved by mechanical
solutions, but through expressions and admissions.
You see, I dwell not in simple speech exchanged with
another, but in a dimension fashioned by palettes of color
and sight, touch and resonance. And for so long I've feared
that any attempt to decipher the riddles of corporeality would
annihilate any mystery behind the enigma of consciousness.

Great joy comes in finally learning how to put some
of the right words to all these transient feelings and
thoughts. But I'm also beginning to acknowledge that the
experiences of life humble our efforts to explicate things.
Isn't it true that some things are better left unexplained?
For theorization about the aches of the
heart will bring you to a brink.
And just beyond this brink, a sea of stars
awaits, shimmering in the dark.
The edge of epistemological certainty.
Here the trail of answers comes to an end.
One realizes that all foundations are built upon
sands that shift and wander like stardust.
All human endeavors are fragile, like the ink
upon a few pages of prolegomena that detail
only portions of a grander history.

Upon this precipice one must make a choice.
You may choose to stay and wonder at the glow of starlight
flooding the waters below and write tomes about it from the
safe security of distance. To take in the beauty from afar
and elude the risks inherent in exploration and proximity.
Or…you may choose to leap out from carefully crafted
observatories into oceans of dangerous magnificence. The
leap is great and the fall is fearful and frightening. But
might I contend that it is *here* and *only* here that we can truly

understand and comprehend the tremendous
pleasures and pains rooted and ingrained
in life's deadliest quests.
Nothing good comes without peril.
Nothing worthwhile is gained by *speaking*
exclusively of love and its sweet dispositions.
To stare into the river of stars is pleasant indeed, but
dreams only come to fruition when one jumps into
the current in search of one irreplaceable light.

But in order to take this leap, you must first
shed your armor for it will sink you.
And yes, without this armor, your heart may be wounded.
You may even perish.
Yet you may also live.
Truly live.
Abandon the illusion of invincibility and
you will gain the inception of reality.

Perhaps artists and poets give us access to
things engineers and astronomers cannot.
Perhaps not.
The brink looms before all.

Therefore I, the hopeless romantic, will
no longer speak in platitudes.
For if I truly am who I abundantly profess to be,

I must cease the theatrics and cast myself again into
the terrible unknown that so fosters my thirst.

For romantics may speak and write of
love for a time or even for an age.
But words devoid of pursuance are oblivion.
Faith without works is dead!

Swim amidst sharks. Fly among angels.
Seek out a star, bright or dim, near or far, and shield
not your eyes from its passion and fervor.
Behold her in all her glory and she shall not avert her gaze
from the scars and tears still fresh upon your flesh.

With new hope now coursing through your veins,
declare in your spirit at last without shame:

"Love is not dead!"
"Love never dies!"

AFTERWORD

LANGUAGE, like art, is sacred. As the final poems within this anthology were puzzled and pieced together, I noticed how the necessary words seemed to trickle in from nowhere. Each riddle of expression was resolved one after another and the finality of this project left me far more content than I'd ever expected. I became transfixed by a newfound appreciation for the linguistic medium. The radical power and *supra*natural nature of language struck me with a realization that I'd taken for granted before. A realization of its therapeutic, communal, and dialogical roles in human existence, both in playful and serious senses. Furthermore, I considered how language could indeed be sacred. In short, language is sacred because it is art. It is expressive. Creative. Filled with an abundance of energy and potential. This begs an additional question. Why is *art* sacred? Allow me to indulge in a little thought exploration. Let's begin with this starting point: all authentic art is at the core, a medium of expression, often between the self and the world. It is, in essence, an attempt to communicate with yourself, with others, and with the transcendent. Because of this, consider language as both magical and mechanical. It unfolds like consciousness or the cosmos, through gradual, accidental emergence *and* guided, essential creativity.

Words are a partial solution to the mystery of otherness and individuality. Like God's grace, the various iterations of language are a gift which we can harness, to ease the profound loneliness of existence and the exquisite suffering attached to life. Like art, the written act is endowed with an aesthetic power. That aesthetic power works in a communicative and medicinal manner, in that it alleviates the alienation of individuality just as physical touch does. Without words, we cannot articulate and define what ails or troubles us. The degree of existential privation we feel is dependent upon our ability to confess, to commune and to communicate with the interior and the exterior world. The seeds of personal despair and depression are trampled when they are given license to proceed from thought to the act of speech. What precisely am I saying, you may ask? Well, that language works in conciliatory and confessional fashions. It laments yes, but simultaneously redresses and gives expression to the countless *whys* and *hows* that life hurls at us. Language (which is *thought* internally), is that still, small, inner voice of the Spirit summoning us beyond reason, towards trust and faith. This trust descends upon our being to touch the fractured self with hope, grace, and meaning. If we embrace these things, we are moved to adopt the pursuit of the Good, which nourishes us with the will to live and to create through self-expression. In the Genesis narrative, God *spoke* and *nothing* became *something*, many things in fact. The creation act was one of self-giving expression, the overflowing wellspring of creativity and majesty. Out of chaos and nothingness emerged artistry—speech—existence. In the face of a personless, suffer-free cosmos, the Creator chose to risk pain and great evil in choosing to create. However, in choosing to speak rather than to remain silent, God chose endless possibility, art, and communication. In the face of our own nihilism, we too must make this choice; to capitulate as life cudgels us into suppressed expression, *or* to make use of the tools we have in order to unfetter and unseal the suffocating, incommunable barrier between the self and the world.

Like Christ, language bridges the gap between the unknowable and the knowable by merging the physical and the metaphysical. It unites the realms of the concrete with the abstract. To speak or to write is in some respects an exorcism of the mystery of Being. In other words, for those like myself, the *telos* (ultimate purpose) of language is found in how it shatters the glass ceiling of life's incomprehensibility and the seemingly incommunicable nature of experience. While there are some things better left in silence (wordless words), it is fundamentally the case that humans ache and yearn and labor in the often-futile hope of describing the unbearably indescribable. This is a negotiation of the distance between you and me, subject and object, divine and human. To harness language in order to do this *is* an act of faith. It presupposes a hermeneutic of trust, *not* of suspicion. This hermeneutic functions as a covenant between the communicant and the recipient, an unspoken promise of good faith. In doing so, the process of linguistic experimentation requests and expects those engaged in communication to adhere by the stipulations of said covenant. The encounter with all art should begin as an act of capitulation where there is no imposition of the self, but rather surrender, as C.S. Lewis firmly remarked.[9] I was reminded of this by the painter Makoto Fujimura, who has observed how the spirit of our age has scuttled our ability to come before art in openness and curiosity. It is ironically the milieu of postmodernism, as Fujimura explains, that has damaged our collective and individual desire to do so. For, "The postmodern art world has come to embrace, or at least acknowledge, that the basis of communication is no longer to be trusted."[10] You see, there are some schools of thought, which are convinced that language is only a tool

9.   C.S. Lewis, *An Experiment in Criticism* (Cambridge: Cambridge University Press, 1992), 18-19.

10. Makoto Fujimura, *Refractions: A Journey of Faith, Art, and Culture* (Colorado Springs, CO: NavPress), 86.

of power, that there is nothing sacred in its interior world, only the stuff that comprises it. In the matter of words, like materialism, there can be no transcendent cause or intention, only the dynamics of hierarchy and suspicion. Some schools of thought go even further, seeking to erase the exchange and interplay between subject and object, or erasing the distinction between the you and the I.[11] All of these ideas are just reincarnated forms of Gnosticism, adapted for a new age. Surely raw material and raw power are not all that exist. Language is more than wordplay *or* ordered hierarchy. Words are holy and incarnational, and they beckon us to search for the truth, beauty, and love that is coded into our very DNA.

I must say that I became a poet mostly by accident or maybe to put it more accurately, by necessity. Poetry began as a series of daily dispatches to channel my cultural and personal weariness. These two categories (the cultural and the personal) became the two overlapping spheres which *Himeros & Anteros* investigated. This project related primarily to the personal, as it truly spanned and encapsulated a lifelong journey of loss and rediscovery. The story and its movement begins in the literal and figurative womb, a sanctuary of innocent wonder and moves through the existential

---

11. This ultimately stems from a spirit of distrust and a rejection that such a thing called human nature exists. The postmodern solution offered is that of self-creation and a posthumanism that, "rejects...the epistemological and ontological groundwork on which the idea of the human evolved, the idea of the "I," the person, as well as language understood as a nexus of relation to and from the world." See Daniel Tobin, *On Serious Earth: Poetry & Transcendence* (Asheville, NC: Orison Books), 90-91.

tomb of a disenchanted and demystified world, with little need for God, and perhaps even someday, love. *Himeros & Anteros* is cultural in its setting, as an idealistic boy navigates the postmodern milieu of Western society. He finds that the annihilation of the metaphysical creates a void which begins to impact relationships, faith, identity, and meaning. Even so, the desire for something beyond a God-less public square initiates a resurrection within. Perhaps this is merely an infantile rejection of the inevitable and the collapse of the old order. Or it may yet be a hope for something more, a synthesis of the old and something yet to be realized.[12]

As I began to close the door on the first revisions of this collection, I went through a phase where I wondered about my own vulnerability and rawness. How would readers perceive my story? Would it be felt as vindictive, trivial, banal, or pretentious? Or would the deep well of my internal hurts, longings, and feelings be sensed on some medial level. For all my efforts, I can only work within the confines

---

12. It was not until this collection had neared its completion that I encountered an article from the Eastern Orthodox theologian, David Bentley Hart. In this illuminating article, Hart thoughtfully summarizes the philosophical (and theological) explorations of Peter Sloterdijk. Like a pathologist of culture, Sloterdijk analyzes the Western sphere of society and the aftereffects of secularism's slow conquest of religion and the seeming departure of God. I was eerily struck by Sloterdijk's declarative autopsies and the similarities that they cast upon my own sensitivities and doubts. Yet still, my spirit, either in willful rebellion, ignorance, or stubborn faith, resolved in futility or maybe in genuine faith that God had not died. Let it not be so. See David Bentley Hart, "No Turning Back: Peter Sloterdijk's *After God*," Commonweal Magazine, July 14th, 2021, https://www.commonwealmagazine.org/no-turning-back-0.

and constraints of language and my own often inadequate skills. There are limits to expression. The common ground between the subjective experience of myself and of the reader, in their interaction with the text, does not necessarily produce a direct correspondence to the objective truth of the events. Unfortunately, the reader can often subvert authorial intention with their own invention. A troublingly common phenomenon in contemporary discourse. The author themselves can also fail to communicate adequately or adeptly. As I elaborated on earlier, the interlocking of these two spheres is not always attainable. However, it is precisely these worries that must be released so that trust and faith can enter. We need faith in the dynamic power of language and trust in the responsible stewardship of the reader. These sentiments are all part of the process of communication. This is when I also noticed the relevant parallel with my healing journey. I imagine most have found that there is a resiliency born when one endures mental and relational trauma. Heartbreak catalyzes all manner of adaptations and growths. It produces a new kind of tenacity and strength that was previously unknown. Beforehand though, you go through a lot of questioning and self-doubt, particularly when you've been caught up in toxic dynamics, emotional manipulation, and dishonesty. So much so, that you begin to second-guess the truth and validity of your own experience. It takes time to sort out fiction from reality, but at some point, you do finally stop doubting yourself. You stop questioning or asking why. You stop harassing yourself. You sever bitterness towards God and towards others. Most importantly you learn to forgive and to accept.

As I shaped and molded additional portions for this work, I began to realize how little time I'd actually given myself to sit in the pain, to truly acknowledge what I'd been through, the things I'd lost. I learned that you must dwell in that pain before it can truly depart. So I finally gave my heart and soul time to grieve. It was that season of lament, if you will, which conceived many of the poems within these pages. I let a great deal flood out. Then those days passed. I began to rediscover a me that had been deposited in the shadows for a long time. I pulled back the curtains veiling my lost self and felt the beauty of life swiftly roar back and with a vengeance. Everything, and I mean *everything*, became more vibrant and verdant. I suppose that was the truest and purest justice I could have found.

Himeros & Anteros, is primarily autobiographical, moving somewhat chronologically through the trials and tribulations of my boyhood imagination, naïveté and young love, and on to maturity, first love, repeated heartbreak, and despair. The repetition of certain thematic elements, like hope, tenderness, waiting, prayer, and dialectical thinking re-insert themselves from time to time in an attempt to establish experiences, principles and overarching themes. As I wrote,

I toiled to write in continuity with the timeless tradition of poetry, probably to an extent that was a bit too flowery and wordy at times. There are hints of numerous historical influences scattered throughout the poems. I drew heavily from the mythological tenor of the Greek pastoral poetry of antiquity which imagines a return to some paradisiacal golden age of tranquility. There are also a host of obscure allusions and references from cinema, literature, and music. These examples, whether they be Miyazaki films or Virgil's Bucolics, represent some of my encounters with beauty and transcendence in the world.

A friend of mine, after reading through a later draft of this collection, said that my poetry was the most *objective* oriented poetry he'd read. I found this interpretation quite humorous and intriguing, especially given the nature of most poetry and the thrust of this particular work, which tends primarily towards the personal. On the level of intention, my friend saw clearly what my spirit had attempted to convey with my literary art. Since my completion of graduate school, I've been grappling with questions about truth and our ability to access and know it. I would often encounter writings in my studies from the postmodernist bent that vehemently eschewed the usage of objective language, and while I could appreciate a degree of this, its absolutism left me unsettled and unconvinced. Ironically, I am of the opinion that a hallmark of good poetry is the ability to create an "aesthetic distance" between subject matter and expression.[13] The idea is that if you speak too directly about an experience or a given topic, something is lost. The poetic flair is diminished. There is a dimension of abstraction or vagueness that creates a necessary degree of separation between content and conveyance. There is faith involved in this. One that trusts that the reader will not float around in the vacuum of meaning that ambiguity can create. In my experience, this trust is usually rewarded, and rewarded deeply. On the other hand, some of the poetry that is felt most primally is the kind that is brutally honest, raw, and direct.

After processing my experiences in writing, I became more attuned to the subjective nature of existence and personal experience. The ambiguity of life, of ethics, and of truth became increasingly relatable to me and began to nuance the idealism I'd once held so tightly to. I found myself nestled somewhere in the middle between the suspicion that postmodernism expresses towards "neutral" ideologies, culturally constructed claims, and unbiased objectivity *and* the classic tradition of faith and its associated creeds. To a certain point, the critical eye that postmodernity brings towards all

---

13. This term is borrowed from Daniel Tobin. I highly, highly recommend reading his *On Serious Earth: Poetry & Transcendence* where he harnesses this term. It will unlock a few ideas hinted at in my poetry, especially for those who have not studied philosophy or theology. I began reading Tobin's book as I was finishing the final poems for this collection. His work brought both clarity and new insight into the last additions I would include, while giving validation to the convictions underlying my written voice. See Daniel Tobin, *On Serious Earth: Poetry & Transcendence* (Asheville, NC: Orison Books), 33.

things is a sort of necessity for true living. It is also a sort of progenitor of doubt and epistemological agnosticism. The doubts that surface are certainly unexpected guests, but not entirely unwelcome ones. I say this because I'm convinced that the purest faith is one that has weathered storms of skepticism. For the faith that emerges on the far side, is one that is mature, nuanced, and fully one's own. A faith continuously interrogated and at times, vindicated. It can even be a wounded faith, increasingly cynical, and bound to newfound aphorisms. This is demonstrated in one of the later poems which rejects divine determinism and clichéd slogans like, "Everything happens for a reason," or "God told me." It jettisons corresponding hierarchies and forms of certitude often associated with an uncritical faith which hasn't truly wrestled with itself or with skepticism. And yet, these realizations did not ultimately lead me into relativism, as maturation led to a new kind of hope and faith, which still accepts revelation and truth, while also acknowledging that we all process and comprehend the world through a limited and situated lens.

The title *The Postmodern Poet*, is ultimately ironic and subversive. This will surely manifest itself in subsequent volumes in *The Postmodern Poet* series, which will address more directly the problems (and positives) that postmodernism is creating in culture and in art. We live in an age largely unmoored from essentialism and timeless truths and yet still embrace them without naming them as such. For no matter how much some may protest, some piece of truth still defines and guides the lives of every human being. The pursuit of meaning, of happiness, of beauty, of love remains universal, even if many have seemingly abandoned such endeavors for a time. But, while the philosophical bent of this collection is certainly pointed in its tenor and convictions, it is still committed to the reality of an individual's uniquely subjective and embodied experience, which is often idiosyncratic.

Although not originally intended, the structure of this collection bears a rough resemblance to the so-called "Hegelian dialectic."[14] Here, there is a sort of simplistic experiential and artistic attestation to the Kantian formula of thesis, antithesis, and synthesis (which Hegel echoed with various formulations of the triad; abstract-negative-concrete).[15] The thesis is rendered in the theological outlook of a boy who holds tightly to a belief in the Divine Hand that cradles the world and His immersion in its goings-ons, including the romantic destiny of said boy. However, the slow march of time and its companions initiate a series of events, experiences and situational junctures which begin to

---

14. One must be careful when using the illusive, often misconstrued and misnamed phrase known as the "Hegelian Dialectic." See Gustav E. Mueller, "The Hegel Legend of 'Thesis-Anthesis-Synthesis," *Journal of the History of Ideas,* vol. 19, no. 3 (June 1958): 411-414; and Kant, Immanuel, *Critique of Pure Reason*, trans. J.M.D. Meiklejohn (Independently published, 2021).

15. G.W.F. Hegel, *The Phenomenology of Spirit*, trans. Peter Fuss and John Dobbins (Notre Dame, Indiana: University of Notre Dame Press, 2019).

erode the edges of a youthful consciousness. The first worldview, that of childlike naïveté, becomes almost entombed within another paradigmatic perspective, the antithesis. Regarded initially as a tumor by the boy, this burgeoning conglomerate of new senses and foreign feelings (rage, lust, cynicism, resignation, and doubt) exhibit the true journey into adulthood and the near destruction and replacement of the thesis with the antithesis. As the anthology draws to its climactic end, the struggle between these two narratives seems to reach a stalemate. At times the thesis prevails, particularly in the *Epilegomena*, while in other instances, the antithesis triumphs, as the *Antilegomena* should make abundantly apparent. Ultimately however, the resolution should be understood dialectically, as the synthesis of the thesis and the antithesis. The final section of *Himeros & Anteros* may be interpreted on the surface as the victory of the youthful dreamer and a depiction of a man who chooses to cling to the same kind of belief and imagination he had when he was younger. And in a sense, this is very much true. For it is declared quite emphatically that "Love is not dead," and by implication, neither is God. Because in the man's embodied experience, the *real*ness of a cosmic being simply won't vanish or dissipate. With this, the end constitutes a refusal to adopt nihilism, simple materialism, or Nietzschean perspectivism for that matter. But this of course comes with a host of new subtleties and nuances, and to be clear, an acknowledgement of the cultural zeitgeist and its significant appeal. For now, the man no longer holds his creeds and hopes with the confidence and ignorance that the boy once did. Now, his faith is somewhat akin to Kierkegaard's leap. Furthermore, doubt and uncertainty are more present than they've ever been. But still, there persists a conviction that love is not dead, because it cannot (and must not) be dead. For if love was dead, all life and living would be utter vanity. Thus, the final line is a declaration of faith and a commitment to trust that this belief will come to an eventual actualization.

In *The Symbolism of Evil*, French philosopher Paul Ricœur outlined a two-fold epistemology that provides another way in which to illustrate the theological journey of *Himeros & Anteros*.[16] As Ricœur explored the relationship between symbols, narratives, myths, language and truth, he proposed two states of reality within which individuals can operate. He simply named them 1st and 2nd naïveté. In 1st Naïveté, the relationship between the self and symbols (a part of reality which points toward the metaphysical or transcendent) is direct and immediate. The symbols are literally real and lived in. Some would assess this worldview as rather childlike and innocent. Ricœur does not concur with that conclusion. Mythology, narrative, archetypes and the supernatural are all intermixed with what we view as objectively true and real. But, as a professor of mine explained, we grow

---

16. Paul Ricoeur, *The Symbolism of Evil*, translated by Emerson Buchanan (Boston, MA: Beacon Press, 1986).

older and experience more of the world, which exposes us to new truths, creating a distance between ourselves and the symbols. As we embrace critical thinking, a gulf is erected, and we move into 2nd Naïveté. In this second state of reality, which is not inherently superior, we begin to understand the limitations of language and being, and that symbols and words are used to point beyond themselves to something else. The literalness of symbolism is no longer embraced as it was before, or at the very least, is embraced in a different fashion. The movement from 1st to 2nd naïveté is often chronological, but not always. Similarly, there is often a fluidity and a fluctuation between these two states, wherein an individual moves back and forth between the 1st and the 2nd over the duration of their existence. My intention in referencing Ricœur here is to illuminate the ways in which childlike idealism relates to adulthood and vice versa. It is my hope that the first volume of *The Postmodern Poet* series will express a journey that many can relate to, perhaps one that is similar to what they've encountered in their own lives. If nothing else occurs for the reader than a new kind of reflection on lost nostalgia that resonates within themselves and on the relationship between the past, present, and future, I will be satisfied. Now, enough of my philosophical ramblings. On to some words of gratitude!

ACKNOWLEDGEMENTS

AT LAST! My first creative writing endeavor has finally come, not merely just to fruition, but more importantly, to completion. I've spent many years outlining, envisioning and composing projects while failing to bring any of them to a conclusion (aside from my academic work). I am hopeful that this anthology will be the first of many future creative publications, whether in poetry or in fiction. The impetus for this particular collection of poems and prose came in the fall of 2019, but really manifested itself during the long months of 2020 and 2021. These were seasons of emotional and relational turmoil. The endurance of the highs and lows which typify romantic pursuits, propelled my mind into many spaces of long and quiet reflection. The clarity I began to find in these moments hardened and defined the resolve of my spiritual and romantic outlooks on life. Those who are closest to me will know the intricacies behind the poems herein and the stories that birthed them. They will know of the darkness, pain, and loneliness that spurred the words as well as the joys, hopes, and dreams put forth. I'm sure a few will grin and chuckle in recognition of this penultimate expression of my romanticism and idealism, because it truly is an authentic and genuine representation of me during my darkest and brightest seasons. At the very least, I hope this anthology will help those who love me understand the inner workings of my fractured and emotive mind and soul. I also hope my words can give voice to others who have felt similarly, like a sojourner in the search for love, meaning, and purpose in this life. There are, of course, a great many people to thank, both indirectly and directly. Each individual has had their own impact on me, no matter how inconsequential, and many cannot be listed here but nonetheless remain dear and near to my heart. Co-workers, fellow students, professors, clergy, and the random and simple individuals one encounters each day, have all left an indelible mark on me.

Firstly, I want to dedicate this to Katherine (*Meema*) Callaghan, my grandmother. One of the first poems I ever wrote came after her passing, and I so wish she was still here to see the completion of one of my dreams. Meema always took great interest in my passion for creativity and in my attempts at writing a novel, so this one's for you, Meema. I miss you so dearly. Mom and Dad. You could not have raised, guided and loved me better than you have. I am astounded by your altruism and sacrificial love every day. You have always been present with me in the tough times. You have planted many of the seeds that have grown into my creative dreams. Thank you, Kaiah and Aleyah, for being friends equally as much as sisters and for enduring my grandiose and verbose ramblings. I love you both so, so much. Grandma and Grandpa. Your unconditional love and support throughout my entire life is unparalleled. There are few people like you. Your love for others goes far beyond the ordinary and your lives of service have shaped the man I am. I apologize for some of the crass language in here! My cousins, aunts and uncles of course! You have all played an immense role in my life, getting me through life by simply being you. I adore each one of you more than you know. A special thanks to my aunt Lori for bringing Good Soil Press to my attention!

To my childhood friends, Samo, Alex, Pablo, and Nick. I will always cherish our friendships even when distance separates us. The memories we've made will never be forgotten. I look forward to sharing in the joys of many more milestones together. A special thanks to Cassie Lefleur for helping with the French and for taking the time to read through the earliest draft, which by the way, was about half the length of the final edition! A special thanks to my fellow peer and poet, Libny Dubreuze, as well. I am deeply grateful for our budding friendship, our philosophical and spiritual conversations, and your insight on many matters. Ian, John,

Bobbie Jo, and Matt. You have all been tremendous in your words of encouragement and insight during times of loneliness and confusion. I cherish each of you! A special thanks to Luke Jennen for taking the time to read through an earlier draft of the manuscript, offering insight and praise as a fellow INFP. This collection is meant to be consumed by idealistic dreamers like us! I'm glad it resonated so deeply with you. Tusen takk! Zach Humpal, your faithful friendship and presence in my life has nuanced my worldview in ways I never quite expected. Thank you for bringing your authentic self to our conversations and bringing your wisdom into my theological and ecclesiastical journeys. I'm glad I sat down next to you in *Intro to World Religions* all those years ago!

There are many others to thank, and I can't name them all, but I'd like to list a number of them. I have so much admiration for my undergraduate professors, Gregory Boyd, Paul Eddy, and Jim Beilby. The contributions that the three of you have made to my faith journey have been truly indispensable. A note of special thanks to David Fredrickson at Luther Theological Seminary for introducing me to the world of ancient Greek poetry, which gave me a great deal of inspiration and insight for this project. Professor Guillermo Hansen, thank you for expanding my ability to think and for entertaining my inquisitive nature. Professor Jennifer Wojciechowski, I appreciate you for being such a voice of nuance and thoughtfulness and for our conversations about the Church. Bryant Kumlin, your friendship at Luther was quite important to me and I cherish who you are, with all your humor and wit. To my Russian pen-pal, Anya, thank you for your deep concern and care for the things going on in my life. You will always have a special place in my heart. Спасибо! The Avignon sisters!! How lucky I am to have had your family's presence in my life at various times. Thank you for being such bundles of joy and love, and Carmelle especially, for being a tender and loving god-sister. To my little, god-brother Genesis, thanks for being one of the most joyous parts of my life these past two years. You are the most precious gift in my life. Life has been rendered infinitely more beautiful by your existence. I'd also like to extend a special thanks to my old BTS compatriots at Bethel, Abbey Kisner, Matt McDonald, and David Felsch, among others. Casa Ruiz, los extraño a todos ustedes. WHC, SOMA, and Sojourners family you all model and reflect the love of Christ like few I know. Sojourners West...words are not enough. I value *each* one of you and each family so very dearly. Thank you for your involvement in my life.

Lastly, to the good folks at Good Soil Press! I cannot describe the pure joy I felt when Steve and Kendal first expressed their serious interest in working with me, I will simply say that I had a very full heart after that conversation! Thank you both for giving me the opportunity to express my vulnerability through the medium of writing and to share myself with others in my first published book. This is a dream I've had since I was a young boy, and you have helped bring that to life. I am grateful for your willingness to see the beauty and possibility in my work. I'd also like to give a significant nod of appreciation to my editor, Heidi Sheard! It takes a great deal of patience and attention to detail to get a project like this to completion. Your encouragement and wisdom were essential in bringing this collection to the place it needed to be. Thank you for seeing the potential here and for advocating for me as a writer! This is an incredible milestone.

Ubi caritas et amor, Deus ibi est.

Josiah Macrae Callaghan
Fall 2022
Minneapolis, Minnesota

CPSIA information can be obtained
at www.ICGtesting.com
Printed in the USA
LVHW030923201122
733280LV00042B/2696

9 781737 039464